EMPLOYEE-PRENEUR

Stephen J. Palmer

Copyright © 2018 Stephen J. Palmer

All rights reserved.

ISBN: 1986947785
ISBN-13: 978-1986947787

DEDICATION

I dedicate this book to all those who have a dream to start, grow, and expand their business. To the entrepreneurs who work a 9 to 5 and a 6 to 12 in their on business. For those who continue to push beyond the fatigue and current situations that are not always pretty. This book is for you!

CONTENTS

	ACKNOWLEDGMENTS	i
	INTRODUCTION	1
1	KEEP YOUR JOB	3
2	SET A GOAL	6
3	MAKE A PLAN	12
4	START WHERE YOU ARE	16
5	RECORD EVERYTHING	18
6	TAKE YOUR TIME	21
7	PAY THE COST	23
8	ENJOY THE JOURNEY	25
9	BE COMMITTMENT	27
10	USE WHAT YOU HAVE	29
11	PREPARE TO SWEAT	32
12	ALLOCATE YOUR MONEY	34
13	MANAGE YOUR ACTIVITIES	37
14	CREATE A ROLODEX	39
15	FIND A MENTOR	43

16	LEARN & BUILD	45
17	KNOW WHEN TO STOP	48
18	TAKE OWNERSHIP	50
19	DO IT FOR FREE	53
20	PRODUCE A TRACK RECORD	55
21	KNOW WHEN TO SAY NO	57
22	SCALE YOUR GROWTH	59
23	HIRE YOUR WEAKNESSES	61
24	NETWORK	63
25	PREPARE FOR YOUR EXIT	66
Bonus	LEAVE THE RIGHT WAY	69
	FINAL THOUGHTS	71
	ABOUT THE AUTHOR	74

ACKNOWLEDGMENTS

I want to thank the many people who not only shared their time but their experiences and resources to help me in my business and have been instrumental in compiling this information. There are so many people to thank and so many people to salute, so without belaboring the point or taking up extra space, THANK YOU FOR ALL YOU DO IN MY LIFE AND IN THE LIVES OF THOSE WHO ENCOUNTER YOUR PRESENCE.

EMPLOYEE-PRENEUR

Stephen J. Palmer

INTRODUCTION

I have discovered that most entrepreneurs are self-employed—they work for their business as an employee. Their goal is to be business owners—the business works for them. However, they find themselves having to work a to take care of their necessities (rent, health insurance, retirement, etc.) Being entrepreneur is not an easy task, especially in the beginning stages. In this simple guide, I outline 25 tips that I have learned in my personal life as well as the information I have obtained from successful entrepreneurs that I have personally known.

Are you an "EmployeePreneur"? What is an employeepreneur? I define an employeeprener as an individual who is employed by someone else but is in the process of starting a business or has started a business on their own. They are employees but are also entrepreneurs. They burn the candle at both ends, working to build their business to someday leave their 9 to 5 job and work on their own.

These tips are not one-size-fits-all. They are laced with principles that stand the test of time and a myriad of situations. Some have been learned through painstaking efforts, while others have been discovered through trial and error. Either way, these principles can help save you time, energy, money, and any frustrations that you may have along the way. I encourage you to take hold of them and start to put them into practice. When applied, these tips can help you move from employee to entrepreneur.

1

KEEP YOUR JOB

Don't quit your job! I repeat, "DON'T QUIT YOUR JOB!" According to the United States Small Business Administration Office, there are 28.8 million small businesses in the United States which represents 99.7 percent of all U.S. Business.[1] Not mention, there has been a continual three-year upward trend in new business startups, with 310 out of every 100,000 adults starting a new business each month.[2]

Now looking at this data, you are probably asking,

---

[1] United States Small Business Profile 2016

[2] 2017 Kauffman Index of Startup Activity

"Why shouldn't I quit my job and go start my business?" Here is why. The United States Bureau of Labor Statistics states that roughly 20 percent of new businesses survive past their first year of operation and around half of all business no longer exist after year five.[3] Another very important thing to consider is that close to 50 percent of businesses fail during the first year in business.[4] One of the major reasons that businesses fail is due to lack of financing. Throughout the U.S. 83% of small business owners financed their own business.[5] And that is hard to do if you don't have the capital.

To save you from being one of the 80 percent of businesses that fail in the first year, mostly due to financing; keep your job! Your goal should be to maximize the job as well as your entrepreneurial opportunities to their capacity. Start building, growing and expanding your business on the side. Think of your

---

[3] U.S. Bureau of Labor Statistics, Business Employment Dynamics

[4] U.S. Small Business Administration

[5] BlueVine Capital Inc.

job as a classroom in which you are getting paid to be there. It is an opportunity for you to plan, prepare and successfully launch your business in the near future!

2

SET A GOAL

What is your goal? Do you have a goal for your business? Earl Nightingale said, "People with goals succeed because they know where they are going." The very first goal should be to determine your purpose. Before moving on take a moment and answer the following questions:

Why do I want to go into business?

What problem or need will my business solve?

As an entrepreneur you will be setting goals, accomplishing them and setting more goals. This why you must become a master at goal setting. Your goals need to be "SMART". S.M.A.R.T. is a mnemonic acronym that means Specific, Measurable, Attainable, Relevant, and Timely. Your goals should not be too vague or broad, but a clear vision that if anyone reads it they can immediately know what to do and what is being accomplished.[6] Below I have included an example to help you come up with S.M.A.R.T. goals.

Let's say you have a goal to sell more of your books.

INITIAL GOAL:

"Sell More Books"

This initial goal is too broad and vague. It leaves room for too many questions and less action. We need to incorporate the S.M.A.R.T. acronym to help us create a more dynamic and motivating goal.

SPECIFIC
"Sell more of my EmployeePreneur book"

Make sure that your goals are well defined and focused. The more focused your goals are, the more focused you

---

[6] Habakkuk 2:2

will be in accomplishing them. Take a look at the below questions to help pinpoint the specific goals you want to reach in your business.

Key Questions:
What am I trying to accomplish? or
Where am I going? In this case,
Which book do I want to sell?

MEASURABLE
"Sell 500 of my EmployeePreneur book"

A goal without a measurable outcome is like playing a game without keeping score. Numbers are essential in business and should be essential in determining your goals. I encourage you to write down your numbers and post them where you can see them every day. Take a look at the below questions to keep you focused on setting measurable goals.

Key Questions:
How will I measure my success?
What quantity or number am I trying to reach?
How many books do I want sell?

> ## ATTAINABLE
> "Sell 500 copies of my EmployeePreneur book online and at each speaking engagement I am invited to"

Dream big, but build small. This is especially true when you are starting out and may not have the necessary resources to do all that you want to do. Your goals should be realistic and something reachable. It is not too small where you do not have to work for it, and it is not to large where you can't do it. At this stage in your journey , set goals that you can accomplish within an 12 months or less time frame. If the industry you are in is not doing 50% don't expect to do 80%. Look at the climate and sector of business that you want to venture in and make sure that you are beyond reality. Look at the questions below and be sure that your goals are attainable for you and your team.

Key Questions:

Is this goal realistic and possible for me to accomplish?
How will I sell my books?
Where will I sell my books?

> ## Relevant
> "Sell 500 copies of my EmployeePreneur book to men and women who are wanting to become entrepreneurs online and at my various speaking engagements"

Your goals should align with your overall purpose and mission. It should be relevant to where you currently are and where you are going. Take a look at the questions below and determine if your goals are relevant.

Key Questions:

Does this goal align with my purpose and mission?
Is this a goal that I must accomplish now or can it wait?
Who does my book help?

> ## Timely
> "Sell 500 copies of my EmployeePreneur book to people who aspire to become entrepreneurs through my online outlets and at my various speaking engagements by the August 1st."

Your goal should have a deadline. It needs a timeframe or time limit to when it must be accomplished. If you fail to put a time on it, your goal becomes just another wish. Think about it like this: When you were in school your teacher would give you an assignment and tell you the due date. Knowing the due date helps you to plan ahead and for when the assignment gets done. Putting a deadline on your goals puts a demand on you to complete them.

Key Questions:

How long will it take me to accomplish this goal?

What specific date or times (if relevant) must this be completed?

When do I want to sell these books?

S.M.A.R.T. Goal:

"I will sell 500 copies of EmployeePreneur to people who aspire to become entrepreneurs through online sales and various speaking engagements by August 1st."

You can use this example to help you set any goal in any area of your life. When you are setting business goals it is always important to not only think about the present environment but also the future outcomes. Setting S.M.A.R.T. goals helps you to work through the process of goal setting, while strategically connecting all the components necessary to help you accomplish your goals.

3

MAKE A PLAN

A plan without a purpose is like breathing without oxygen. You can't do it and you probably shouldn't try. Some people make plans without having a real purpose, and this becomes one of their major downfalls and frustrations in business. In the previous chapter, you wrote down your purpose and defined some goals. In this chapter, you will put legs on the goals by planning on what needs to be done.

Making a plan is taking the time to determine the necessary actions that need to take place to make your goals a reality. Though we are planning in the present, while you are working your current job, we are focused on the future and what we intend to accomplish. Alan Lakein put it this way, "Planning is bringing the future into the present so that you can do something about it."

Take moment and pull out your goals and a calendar. Imagine yourself accomplishing each goal (what it will feel like, look like, and all the things you can do once you accomplish these goals). Now, mark your deadlines on the calendar and count how many days from today you to complete your goal. This becomes your timeframe for constructing a well-designed plan.

When designing your plan you will work with the end in mind. This means that each day you will create a task to help you accomplish your goal by your set deadline. Let's look at the below example:

GOAL:
"I will sell 500 copies of EmployeePreneur to people who aspire to become entrepreneurs through online sales and various speaking engagements by August 1st."
DEADLINE:
Wednesday, August 1, 2018
DAYS TO COMPLETION:
125

DAY 1:   Create a landing page on my website for customers to purchase a hard copy or e-book online.
DAY 2:   Create a Social Media Ad for my book and link it to my website.
DAY 3:   Create 3 hashtags and ask 10 of my closest friends to share my post on their page.
DAY 4:   Order 100 hard copies of my book for my upcoming speaking engagement.
DAY 5 – 124:   …Whatever other tasks that need to be complete
DAY 125:   500 copies of my book sold   (Online Sales: 350 copies and Speaking Engagements: 150)

Since there are 125 days for me to complete this task I can break up the task on certain days. For example, every Monday and Wednesday I will work on completing at least two the tasks listed. Or you may want to only work a Monday-Friday schedule on these tasks and rest on the weekend. Whatever you decide make sure that you don't let a week go by from working on your goals. After all, this is your business and if you don't work on it, who will?

If you noticed, each day leading up to my goal due date

will be filled with specific, "bite-sized" tasks that I can do while still working my job. The plan is a living document and may be changed or adjusted as you go along. The focus is to plan your work then work your plan each day.

By breaking your goal into doable daily tasks, it helps you from burning out and keeps you making progressive steps toward starting, growing, and expanding your business.

4

START WHERE YOU ARE

Most people wait for everything to be perfect before they begin. They are waiting for all their "ducks to be in a row" and wanting to have everything they need before they make the first move. In hindsight, this method is not the best. If you sit and wait too long you will miss opportunities, trends, and fluctuations in your particular business sector that could be very beneficial. Think of it this way,

> **"People who won't take step number one never take step number two."**
> Zig Ziglar

Sometimes beginning is the most difficult part of starting a business. This is especially true when you begin to think about all the potential challenges and uncertainties you may face as an entrepreneur.

If you've been procrastinating commit to completing the first step or the next step in starting, growing, or expanding your business. You may be surprised how much more do-able being an entrepreneur seems after you simply start it.

5

RECORD EVERYTHING

Dream it, develop it, do it, then document it; In that order! These are the words of one of my mentors and these words stuck with me since the moment he spoke them. I am an avid believer that a short pencil is better than a long memory, so it if very important that we write everything down.

As an entrepreneur it is good for you to keep record of the various things that you do in your business. I encourage you to keep a time card of when you work on your business, where you work, and the mileage, if any that is traveled. This information becomes useful not only during tax season but also as data you can use to track your growth and patterns.

Think of your notes as a recipe card that you can come back to later when you want to know how to do make a special dish. When you record your activities, your processes, and the various systems that you use, this can become your future employee manual, operating procedures, and a host of other valuable information compiled for your keeping.

Here are some suggested things you should record:

- New Ideas
- Finances (every penny you spend)
- Mileage Log
- How To Procedures
- Industry Facts, Statistics, and Trends
- Clients
- Important Websites
- Important Numbers

- Important

Depending on how you like to do things, I would recommend using folders or creating folders on your computer in which you can scan and store these documents in.

6

TAKE YOUR TIME

Most people want things quick, fast and in a hurry. You may be at your job and things are not going like you hope or expect them to be. You are ready to move on; ready to start your business and just up and leave. However, did you ever think that maybe taking your time is more beneficial than you think?

Patience is not just a virtue but a strategy. The strategy is implemented when you take your time to pace yourself. You want to have endurance and build a business that will be able to sustain you and those you love. Moving too quickly can hurt you and cause you to miss key steps and make hasty decisions that can lead to negative outcomes.

Taking your time does not mean you procrastinate and never start (See Chapter 4). This means you intentionally work at a diligent and timely pace. You do what is necessary even if it means going at a slower pace than what you like. Remember,

> ***"Success does not happen overnight.***
> ***It happens overnights."***

Learn to pace yourself and take the time your time to grow and thriving and successful business.

7

PAY THE COST

Entrepreneurs must be willing to pay the cost in order to start, grow, and expand their business. The cost you pay cannot be avoided. Below is a list of costs that entrepreneurs must pay:

- **Time** – there will be nights and days you may have to lose sleep in order to work on or for your business.

- **Money** – it takes money to make money. Money is a seed that must be planted in order to receive more of it.

- **Work** – if you don't work, you don't eat. Work is a necessary activity for any and all entrepreneurs. (See more in Chapter 11).

- **Comfort** – entrepreneurship will often cause

you to step out of your comfort zone in order to see a task through to the end.

- **Associations** – not everyone can go with you and not everyone will go with you. You may lose old friends because you are working toward a goal and their negativity becomes a hindrance.

- **Leisure** – as you start, grow and expand your business you will have to be willing to give up times of leisure (just for a season) in order to use that time and those resources to go toward your entrepreneurial goals.

These are just a few of the more apparent cost that is associated with being an entrepreneur. Often times as an EmployeePreneur, you will have to pay a little more in cost because you don't work full-time in your business as someone who does. But don't be discouraged. When you pay the cost you reap the reward.

> **"Success is no accident. It is hard work, perseverance, learning, studying, sacrifice and most of all, love of what you are doing or learning to do. "**
> **Pele**

8

ENJOY THE JOURNEY

So many people are caught up in the destination, that they miss the benefits and beauties on the journey. The road journey from employee to entrepreneur can have touch moments and sacrifices (See Chapter 7), but there are also some beautiful moments, memories and benefits that come along with that journey.

Having a passion and love for what you do is a vital key to enjoying the journey. As you start, grow, and expand your business, learn to look at the brighter side of things and not always the negative. See the beauty in the lessons you learn, the cost you pay, and the value of the clients you help. Never let the stress or the sweat of the work, cause you to miss out on the beauty of the moment. Greg Anderson put it this way, "Focus on the journey, not the destination. Joy is found in finishing an activity but in doing it."

9

BE COMMITTMENT

Whenever I think about commitment, I think about the story of the chicken and the pig. One morning at a local farm a chicken and a pig were reading the morning newspaper. On the front page of the newspaper in big bold letters, they read the headline: "Orphanage In Need Of Food!" The chicken noticed that the orphanage was nearby and so she came up with a bright idea. She turned to the pig as said, "Brother big, why don't we go down to that orphanage and make a donation of food? "We can provide them with a ham and egg breakfast!" Now the pig was greatly disturbed and turned to the chicken and said, "For you, that is just a contribution, for me, that requires a total commitment."

This is a funny story with a relevant lesson. Most people think that because they make a contribution that they are fully committed. That is not always the case. I can make a contribution without being committed, but I cannot be committed without making a contribution.

You have probably given to various charities or even given money to someone you did not know was in need of assistance. Your giving was a contribution of money or resources, but it was not a commitment. Like the pig in the above story, commitment requires you to put your life into the cause (time, energy, money, etc.).

As an entrepreneur, you must be committed. If you don't give it 100% you won't get what you desire. Here are a few things you should be committed to:
- Your Purpose – (Chapter 2)
- Your Plans (Chapter 3)
- Your People (Chapter 23 & 24)
- Paying the Cost (Chapter 7)
- Completing the Journey (Chapter 8)

Once you give it 100% you'll get what you're looking for.

10

USE WHAT YOU HAVE

If you are like me, you have probably heard it said once or twice, "Use what you have to get what you want." The same is true as an EmployeePreneur. You must learn to utilize what you do have in order to get what you want.

Being resourceful and producing big results from small means is crucial to any entrepreneurs' long-term success. Do not focus on what you don't have, focus on what you do have. Most people wait for things to be perfect and have all their "ducks in a row". But what happens when you don't have all the ducks? Will this stop you from moving forward? You have to learn how to make do with what you have. As you continue to learn and grow you can obtain the things you need, but never discount what you already have.

Here are some things you probably did not know you have:

- **Information** – you have access to information via many modes of technology.

- **Skills/Talents** – you are an expert in things that you probably discount as being valuable. Learn to monetize your skills and talents.

- **People** – there are individuals you know and who know you that are willing to help you in whatever way they can.

- **Passion** – is a deep love for your dream and goals to see them accomplished.

- **Energy** – you need the energy to get things

done. It is the fuel to your actions.

- **Ideas** – need often breeds the creativity because you have to do things out of necessity; you don't always have the luxury of going to buy something.

- **Time** – use your time wisely and maximize it to get the most value for it.

You have more than you know, so it's time you start using what you have. It is never a lack of money or resource, just ideas. You will not always be in a place of limited resources however, you can never gain the needed resources if you don't use what you have.

Take it from a man who was no stranger to success in his field, Arthur Ash:

> **"Start where you are.**
> **Use what you have.**
> **Do what you can."**

11

PREPARE TO SWEAT

Work! Yes, for some it is a four-letter curse word, for others, it is a friend and way to escape. For an entrepreneur, it is a way of life. As a matter of fact, 63 percent of small business owners work between 40-59 hours a week.[7] When you factor in that a full-time employee works 40 hours a week, you can only imagine how many hours an EmployeePreneur must work.

---

[7] TAB Work-Life Balance Survey of Small Business Owners

We will dive more into your time in Chapter 13. For now, I want to focus on the reality that you must prepare to sweat. This means you will have to work, work, work some more, and work even harder to start, grow and expand your business.

You are going to have to 'roll-up-your-sleeves' and work every aspect of your business. This is not always easy being that you will be working another 40 or so hours as an employee at another job. As an EmployeePreneur, you will have to burn the candle at both ends. Work your job with excellence and candor (See Chapter 18) then work your business with the same level of intensity when you're off.

Keep in mind, "Work is good!" you don't magically wake up and have all your dreams come true. Success requires work, and every successful entrepreneur knows that.

12

ALLOCATE YOUR MONEY

Did you know that 60 percent of small business owners used their personal funds to start, grow, and expand their business?[8] Another 48 percent went without pay, and 17 percent delayed major expenses such as payroll or rent.

Cash flow challenges continue to be a hurdle for new and growing businesses. After all, "Cash is King"! it is one of the major indicators of the health of a business. So, it must be vitally important that you are able to make sound financial decisions with your money. The

---

[8] BlueVine Capital Inc.

word "allocate" is a financial and economical term that means to distribute resources into shares or portions. It is a more direct and intentional approach to budgeting.

You must be intentional about your money. As an EmployeePreneur, you have the benefit of working as an employee that receives a paycheck and as an entrepreneur who can fund their business from the paycheck you receive as an employee. The earned income you make from working should be converted into an infusion of capital for your business. The amount of money you put into your business is up to you.

In the classic novel *"The Richest Man in Babylon"* by George S. Clason, one of the main characters, Arkad, gives *7 Cures to a Lean Purse.* On this list, he instructs his class to do the following:

"Put each coin to laboring that it may reproduce its kind even as the flocks of the field and help bring to the income, a stream of wealth that shall flow constantly into thy purse."

He explains that once you started saving at least 10

percent of what you earn, you must put that money to work. This same principle is true as an EmployeePreneur. Each paycheck you receive from your job should have a portion allocated to your business. By proactively setting a percentage of your earned income aside for your business, you give yourself an advantage by being prepared (See Chapter 25) for the inevitable capital you will need in the near future.

Start now while you are still working to set aside capital for your business. allocate your money by turning your earned income into a portfolio and a passive income. Use the money from your employment to build the business.

13

MANAGE YOUR ACTIVITIES

Your most valuable asset is not money or knowledge. It is time! Entrepreneurs are pulled in hundred directs and wear many hats with. As you start, grow, and expand your business you will be involved in a lot of research, networking, planning, business strategy, marketing, sales, all while still working your 9 to 5.

As a result, entrepreneurs have to jump between task and the 24 hours in a day can seem too little in order to accomplish all you have to do. This is why time management is an essential, especially as an EmployeePreneur.

When I talk about time management, I am not talking just talking about putting things on your calendar. In all fairness and honesty, I don't believe that you can manage time, you can only manage the activities that you do within the time you are given.

As you start, grow or expand your business, you will need to determine what things need to be done in the time you have after work (See the Book Stop, Continue, Start). Balancing a job and your business is a great practice that requires: attention, focus, energy, and scheduling. Knowing how to prioritize and schedule things so that they work WITH you instead of against you is key. Keep in mind that your greatest asset is time and depending on your business it will require a lot more of it. I suggest working your job and setting aside time to work on your business. Remember you are not running a sprint but a marathon, so it is okay to go slow, as long as you are going in the right direction.

14

CREATE A ROLODEX

Yes, I am a millennial. And yes I do know what a rolodex is. For those you who were born after me, a rolodex is a desktop card index used to record names, addresses, and contact information for contacts. Whether you use the "old school" desktop rolodex or you create an electronic rolodex, as an entrepreneur it is important to have a list of people you can call and count on.

Think of your contacts like your business team. They

may not actually receive a 1099 or W-2 but they are individuals that can help to advise you or that you can call on to get pertinent information when starting, growing, or expanding your business.

These individual can be friends, colleagues or associates who have a wealth of knowledge in a particular area, where you may be lacking. They can be business owners or just regular employees. Either way, they can provide a knowledge, skill or insight for minimum or no cost to you. Here is a list of people you should have in your rolodex. If you fit the criteria, you can fill the next position with someone who does not have your skill set.

- **Attorney** – for the legal side of business and compliance with particular laws and governances.

- **Accountant** – for the financial side of business and keeping your cash in order.

- **Web Designer** – in today's society, if you don't have a website you are not in business.

- **IT Professional** – technology is not only the way of the future it is in every industry and sector today. You need someone that can help you troubleshoot and know certain programs/apps that can assist you in starting, growing, and expanding your business.

- **Banker** – this is your go-to person for business banking. They know the type of accounts to open for your business, what type of loans, credit cards, and all other banking services for your business.

- **Other Business Owners** – birds of a feather not only flock together but go in the same direction. You want to surround yourself with people who can provide inside into particular opportunities and deals that you may have. These individuals know business and can help you navigate through new terrain (See Next Chapter).

This is not an exhaustive list but it is a great starter. Other individuals you may want to have would be business consultants, those in marketing, social media specialist, and industry experts in your business sector. The advantage of a rolodex is that you have a relationship with people who are experts and who are willing to help you and you move from employee to entrepreneur.

15

FIND A MENTOR

Do you have a mentor? If not it is very important to have someone or even a group of people in your life that can help you see what you can't and help you go to the next level as an entrepreneur. Junot Diaz put it this way, "Colleagues are a wonderful thing – but mentors, that's where the real work gets done."

It is vitally important that you have someone that can help you as you make your transitions from employee to entrepreneur. They don't have to be in the same industry, but they should have a track record of running a successful business or company. "Where there is no counsel, the people fail; But in the multitude of counselors there is safety."[9] Without wise advice, you can expect to fail, especially if you do not know what you are doing. As an EmployeePreneur, you should make it a common practice to learn from other entrepreneurs. Learn to make their failures your successes and their successes your success.

A good place to start finding a mentor would be looking at your Rolodex (See the Previous Chapter). These individuals become your coach on this journey to business ownership. You want to soak up their knowledge and expertise because they have been where you want to go. You can glean from the journey in order to leverage the wisdom they had to learn the hard way. This will give you the advantage of saving time and avoiding pitfalls that you probably would not have seen if they were not in your life.

---

[9] Proverbs 11:14 New King James Version

16

LEARN AND BUILD

75.4 percent of successful entrepreneurs worked as employees at other companies for more than 6 years before launching their own business.[10] 96 percent of successful entrepreneurs say that prior work experience is an important factor for success in business.[11] So why is this important?

Working as an employee you are gaining a knowledge of how things work in a business or maybe how things

---

[10] Founder Institute

[11] Ewing Marion Kauffman Foundation

should not work. Entrepreneurs are always looking for ways to improve things (See Chapter 18). And what better way than to get paid for learning what to do or what not to do in your own business.

Your prior and current work experience becomes your track record for the knowledge that you will need in running your business. No matter what level you are on in your current company or what sector you are in, you are learning valuable skills and gaining knowledge that will be useful in some shape or form, for your business.

While you work your job learn all you can and take advantage of the opportunities (paycheck, training, new information, etc.) that your employer provides. While you work your job, build your infrastructure for your business by applying what you have learned on the job. Don't be afraid to ask your coworkers questions about what they do and begin implementing things you learn in your business.

Make it a point to learn something new about your employer that can help you grow your business. every week doing something to grow and develop the Stop

Discounting job as a timewaster. Look at your job as a learning platform and stepping block to help you reach your goal or becoming a business owner. Don't be discontent, be deliberate and determined to learn all you can so that you can build a better business.

As an EmployeePreneur, your 9 to 5 is the classroom, and you're getting paid to be there. Your "real job" starts after the 9 to 5 ends.

17

KNOW WHEN TO STOP

A study published online in the International Small Business Journal revealed that although persistence is a key to business success, entrepreneurs should know when to abandon a business and find something that provides a greater opportunity if they want to be more profitable.[12]

You must know when to stop pursuing your particular business endeavors if you truly want to be a successful entrepreneur. Knowing when to stop is just as important as knowing when to start. If you continue to

---

[12] SAGE Publishing

pursue your business goals when you should stop and rethink your plans, you can find yourself in an emotional, physical, and financial distress.

Don't think of stopping as a failure. There is a difference. Stopping for the right reason is called, "making a wise decision." Here are some reasons to stop working on your business.

1. **Time** – if you find yourself unable to devote the time needed to start, grow, or expand your business you need to consider stopping.

2. **Money** – if money is becoming a burden or a drain on you and your family's livelihood, you need to consider stopping.

3. **Passion** – if you lose passion or your drive for your particular business you need to consider stopping. You don't want to do something that you don't love especially if it is your own business. become a burden you give up based on the.

When you stop for the right reasons, it is not quitting. It is making the right decision now so that you and all those you love can benefit from your decision later.

18

TAKE OWNERSHP

One of my mentors tells the story of his father who was a successful businessman. He would observe his father in various aspects of the business and learned a lot from what he saw. On this particular day, he saw his father leave a piece of trash at the entrance of the business before he walked through the door. When his father walked in he greeted everyone and headed to his office to conduct an interview with the candidate who was already waiting in the lobby. After the interview, his father intently watched as the interviewee walked out the entrance door. The interviewee unknowingly headed walked to their car and drove off without ever noticing that my mentor's father was watching. When the interviewee drove off, my mentor's father would say to the receptionist, "Remove them from the hiring list." My mentor watched his father continue to do the same thing for each candidate that came in until finally, a candidate walked out of the entrance door but and immediately came back in holding the piece of trash in their hand to dispose of it. My mentor's father hired that person on the spot. When he asked his father why he chose that candidate, his father stated, "I want people who work here to take ownership of our business. "Everywhere from the parking to the warehouse is a representation of who we are. "I want them to treat their job like their own business. "A person who is willing to bend down and pick up trash at their job is a person you can trust to take responsibility."

Do you take ownership at your job? Do you treat your job like you would treat your own business?

You must always remember the principle that you will reap what you sow.[13]

Just as committed as you are to your business you should be committed to working with excellence and doing your best. You never want to burn bridges or produce negative seeds that can affect your business and those you love.

In the words of Zig Ziglar,

"You can have everything you want in life if you just help enough people get what they want in life."

After all, business is all about helping to meet the needs of your clients. What better place to start than at your current job.

---

[13] Galatians 6:7 New King James Version

19

DO IT FOR FREE

Find something you love to do, that you will do it for free, but you do it so well that you get paid for it. Who would not want to live a life where you have found what you are passionate about and now you get to do it, on top of that, you get paid for it! Do it for Free.

When you are first starting out in business it is good to have references. One of the ways you build those references is by providing your service or product for free. Yes! I said free! Remember you are planting a seed for more and better to come. Starting out everyone is not going to know the value or quality of your business. Potential clients may not even know who you are. One of the best ways to gain word of mouth marketing, and test your services or products is by giving it away for free.

Take it from Napolean Hill, the author of "Think and Grow Rich",

"The man who does more than he is paid for will soon be paid for more than he does."

20

PRODUCE A TRACK RECORD

A track record is based on your past performance, achievement, and or failures. A track record shows clients that you can do what you said and you can and have the proof. Your job becomes your track record.

When was the last time you looked at your a current job description? I encourage you to do a search using your current and even past job descriptions. Take a look at the job duties, responsibilities, requirements, and skills preferred. Now think about the tasks and projects you have worked on and how you helped your current employer. Write down what you think about and utilize the words listed in the job description to describe the previous work you have performed for your employers. This is your track record.

Your prior duties, responsibilities, tasks, and projects are your track record for your business. This becomes your proof that you can and have done the work that needs to be done.

Entrepreneurs know how to maximize their current positions in order to monetize their future opportunities.

21

KNOW WHEN TO SAY NO

Psychology Today had an online article by Dr. Judith Sillis entitled, "The Power of No". This article transcribed, "Wielded wisely, No is an instrument of integrity and a shield against exploitation. "It often takes courage to say. "It is hard to receive. But setting limits sets us free."[14]

Knowing when to say no is an instrument that helps you to stay focused on what your goal is and creates a barrier to taking on too much at one time. Remember you are an EmployeePreneur and your time, energy and

---

[14] www.pyschologytoday.com

money is valuable. You can't afford to do everything so you must be prepared to say no even when you may not want to. Below are some things you should say "No" to.

1. Timewasters
2. Wrong Timing
3. Frivolous Spending
4. Non-Essential Activities
5. Giving Up
6. Failure
7. Fear
8. Negative People
9. Negative Things
10. Shortcuts

When you are focused on your building your business you can easily say no to the things that can delay you from starting, growing, and expanding your business.

22

SCALE YOUR GROWTH

Scaling a business means setting the stage to enable and support growth in your business. This requires planning, capital, the right systems, processes, and technology so that you have the capacity and capability to handle growth.

You must take an honest look at your business and ask yourself the question if you are ready for growth. More growth means more responsibility. With more responsibility, there is more work. You must be prepared to handle the growth that you desire. Growing too fast too early can be stifling to your business if you are not ready for the growth.

As you are starting out think about what working on your business not just in it. Here are some points to remember as you scale your growth.

- Be committed to growing your business.
- Determine what amount of growth you can handle.
- Define your processes and systems for operating.
- Choose a Strategy
- Stay abreast of technology
- Connect with the right people
- Ask for Help
- Measure your results.

Scaling your business can help you move from $0 to $1,000. From $1,000 to $10,000. From $10,000 to $100,000. From $100,000 to $1,000,000. Growth is all based on you and what you are willing to do. Successful entrepreneurs understand that growth is intentional and that you must be willing to do whatever it takes to prepare yourself to handle that growth.

23

HIRE YOUR WEAKNESSES

As your business grows, you will grow with it. However, you can't do everything and you should not do everything. A successful entrepreneur knows when to say "No" (See Chapter 21) and knows when to delegate or hire someone to come it to do what they can't.

Some people don't feel the need to hire because they can "YouTube" or "Google" the information to learn how to do it themselves. Conversely, you should already have enough tasks and responsibilities on your plate; in which you don't need to try to take on any more. Remember, time is your greatest asset and you must learn how to maximize your time and get the best quality for your work by hiring those who know what you don't and can do what you are unable to.

A great place to start looking for people to hire would be your Rolodex (See Chapter 15). You can begin by hiring these individuals as contractors to help you with large projects or important tasks. Because you already have a rapport with them and trust them, you will not have to worry about the caliber of their work. Learn to lean on the resource you have in the expertise of others and watch how you maximize your time and give yourself peace of mind.

When your business continues to grow and it is time to hire other employees, go back to your Rolodex (See Chapter 15) and contact your attorney and account to make sure that you are in compliance with State and Federal Laws. Make sure that you take care of those financially that take care of you with their knowledge and expertise. Entrepreneurs that hire their weakness, strengthen their weaknesses while positioning their business for short-term and long-term growth.

24

NETWORK

Take a moment to think about this quote:

> **"If your business comes from relationships, relationships should be your business."**
> **Doug Ales**

No matter where you go, you will have to deal with people. Successful entrepreneurs know that people are customers, employees, and partners. People are the reason your business exists and will continue to exist because you are providing "people" with a product or service. This is why it will behoove you as an EmployeePreneur to get to know people on your job and in your industry.

Networking is the practice of mutually connecting people with people in order to build a professional relationship that can be beneficial to your business goals. Now, I am not suggesting that you just network with people to get something from them or use them for what they can do for you.

Networking has many benefits and can afford you the opportunity to exchange ideas, enrich your life, enhance your business and meeting new and interesting people. There is a myriad of ways to network, but here are a few everyday places you may attend or could attend.

- Company Functions
- Industry Meetings (seminars, conference, etc.)
- Local Chamber of Commerce
- Alumni Events
- Local Small Business Administration Office
- Church
- Professional Mixers (Meet new people and find industry professionals)

Never forget, that who you know is just as important as what you know because what you know does you no good if you are not in front of the right people.

25

PREPARE FOR YOUR EXIT

You don't get what you want in life, you get what you prepare for. If you want to leave your employment and move full-time into being an entrepreneur, you must prepare for the leave. One of the best ways to be ready for the next level is to prepare for it on your current level.

It can be tempting and you can grow anxious to leave your current employment at various times. However, you do not want to prematurely leave and not be prepared for the realities of being an entrepreneur.

Knowing when to leave is just as important as knowing what you are leaving to. The goal of an EmployeePreneur is to build your business while you are working, so when you do leave, you are ready to leave at the right time.

A good rule of thumb for knowing when to leave is to look at your income. Your money should be a primary indicator if and when you should leave. A common practice that many entrepreneurs have told me is "Once your business is making twice your salary, quit your job." Here are some useful indicators that should be in place before you leave your employer. No, all these tips may be relevant to you, but they can serve as a helpful gauge when making your decision to leave.

1. The Net Income of your business should match or exceed your current salary.

2. You have enough money saved to support you and your family.

3. You have an above average credit score.

4. You are able to pay your bills up for at least six

months.

5. You have a resolve in your heart to be committed to the business no matter what happens.

Don't rush the process. Trust the purpose and stay the course. When it's time to move from employee to entrepreneur you will know. Each day you work on your goals and prepare to leave, you are moving closer and closer to that time.

(Bonus)
26

LEAVE THE RIGHT WAY

Your business is making more for you than your current salary. You have enough money saved in your personal account and in your business to sustain your move. You have talked it over with your family and mentors and you are wholeheartedly committed to seeing your business thrive. Now the time is right for you to leave. You will drop off the "employee" from EmployeePreneur and become an entrepreneur.

How should you do it? Should you just walk out,

give the boss and a few co-workers a piece of your mind? Should send a letter? The Grand Finale can make a big difference. The ultimate test to you individually and as a business person is to be able to leave your job the right way. How you end a thing is how you begin a thing. Recall, you are sowing seed for the future right here in the present. What you do and how you react can come back to help you or haunt you. Think about this, some of the people you leave could be your future clients or maybe future employees. What you do until you leave is critical.

I know that you are excited and ready to make your move. However, I suggest you use wisdom and an elegant candor to your exit. Be professional and courteous to each person. Let it be known that you are thankful for the lessons and opportunities that you've had and will be utilizing what you have learned to start, grow and expand your business.

FINAL THOUGHTS

Practicing these tips can help build a solid foundation for you and your business. Your planning, balancing, timing, and commitment is essential in order to move through the process of becoming a full-time business owner and not just an employee.

The question now becomes do you have the basic skills to see to it that you put these tips into practice? No matter how rigorous or draining working your job and building your business may be, you must to be willing to make the sacrifice. It will take a lot of time management and focus. Dedicating at least an hour a day to your business will not only keep you motivated about your dreams but it will continue to place you a step closer every time to your goals.

Success comes in pieces. Every day you work, every day you learn, every day you build you are living out what most people only wish they could. Yes, you have a 9 to 5 right now, but in the near future, you will be a successful business owner. For now, as you build you will be and EmployeePreneur.

EMPLOYEEPRENEUR

ABOUT THE AUTHOR

Stephen Palmer began his public service career a decade ago with the Marshal's Department in Fulton County. Over the years, he received the Gold Medal of Commitment for Excellence in Professionalism & Justice for his leadership role in various charity and office comradery events. Joining the U.S. Department of Homeland Security, he graduated top of his class as an Immigration Enforcement Agent and was later appointed Chief of Staff to Georgia's District 62 and served as the Special Projects Coordinator for Georgia's Criminal Justice Coordinating Council. Most recently, Stephen served as the executive pastor of Church of the Harvest Fayetteville in Fayetteville, Georgia. He is a sought-after speaker, organizational trainer, and the author of Stop, Continue Start (2012), The Pillars 4 Success (2013), Now & Later: Social Skills for Today's Youth (2015), and He Rose: A Daily Inspirational (2017). Stephen's messages reach a large genre of audiences and centers around the fundamental premise: know God and fulfill your purpose. As a proud husband to his wife Alexis, and new father to his daughter Grace, Stephen balances his time to teach, train, and minister to countless people throughout the country and abroad.

EMPOWER YOUR LIFE!

Whether you are starting a business, working toward a goal or making moves in the corporate world, J. Stephen Palmer's resources will help prepare you to live an empowered and impactful life.

Stop Continue Start
In this easy to follow and fill-in the blank reading, you will learn how to properly evaluate your life so that you can elevate your life by accomplishing your goals.

Shine the Light (Audio)
To elevate your life you must properly evaluate your life. Stephen gives a practical easy to apply message on how to evaluate your life in order to elevate your life to where God wants you to go.

The Pillars 4 Success
It is easy to gain knowledge but it is not easy to stay consistent in apply what you learn. In this action oriented book, you will learn the pillars necessary to turn your knowledge into action and action into success.

Distractions (Audio)
You cannot avoid distractions, but you can dismiss them. Stephen shares with us how to detect and dismiss the distractions in our life that keep us from fulfilling our purpose here on the earth.

HE Rose
Jesus' resurrection has many benefits and blessings that are meant to help us live this life more abundantly. Take this daily journey in discovering who Jesus is and how His life can be a daily inspiration to yours.

Are you Available (Audio)
Stephen breaks down how God is not looking for you to have the most ability, but looking to see if you are willing and available for Him to use.

Don't Trust The Process
Stephen encourages us to refocus our attention, attitudes, and actions on the purpose of the process and how to make the most of every moment by leaning on the One who created the process.

GROW UP PT. 5 (Audio)
Stephen continues Part 5 of this profound series on maturing by learning how to endure through the difficult moments in life. The best is yet to come when you are willing to endure to the end.

Call (678) 948 5769 order online at www.jstephenpalmer.com

www.ingramcontent.com/pod-product-compliance
Lightning Source LLC
Chambersburg PA
CBHW070204230526
45471CB00002B/817